My Very Own

Poetry Collection

101 Poems for
First Graders

by Betsy Franco

Teaching Resource Center

For Janis Poe who makes all my books look beautiful

Heartfelt thanks to Triona Gogarty and Diane McCoy, two wonderful
first grade teachers who gave me terrific advice, and to Debbie Diller
for her invaluable feedback and her constant encouragement

Published by
Teaching Resource Center
14525 SW Millikan, #11910 Beaverton, OR 97005-2343
1-800-833-3389
www.trcabc.com

Design and production by Janis Poe
Illustrations by Linda Starr
Edited by Laura Woodard

Printed in the United States of America
ISBN: 1-56785-062-6

Table of Contents

Introduction

Poetry is a perfect way to introduce first graders to the various stages of literacy. It's short. It's fun. It's got rhythm!

The poems in this personal poetry collection have been carefully crafted to meet the specific needs of first graders. Themes and topics used by most first grade teachers are the focus of the collection. There are sets of poems about *Getting to Know Me, School Stuff, Part of a Community,* and *My Country and My World.* There are *Math Poems, Science Poems,* and *A Lot About Animals* Poems. *That Time of Year* includes poems about the seasons, the weather, the months, and the holidays. *Goofy Poems* round out the collection with a few good laughs.

The poems in the collection are from four to ten lines long. Those within the beginning themes are simpler. They include many high frequency words that children can use as anchors, and there is a great deal of repetition to make the poems more predictable. The vocabulary and language of the poems become progressively more complex with each theme, but there are plenty of high frequency words throughout.

Reading a poem in many forms makes it fun for first graders to practice and develop their literacy skills. For individual, group, and whole-class work, we've provided the tools you need. Each poem has a student poem page with an engaging illustration. These pages make it easy for children to create their own personal poetry collections. For group and center work, we've provided strips to use with the Desktop Pocket Chart. We've also included instructions for enlarging the poems for use as poetry posters.

Versatility

There are enough poems in the collection to present at least two per week. You can use the poems in order or you can choose according to the themes your class is studying. You can also focus on poems that enhance a particular math, social studies, or science lesson.

The section on math poems include such topics as time, money, shapes, one hundred, subtraction, and pre-multiplication.

Social studies topics appear under *School Stuff, Part of a Community,* and *My Country and My World.*

Science poems present the following topics: gravity, parts of a plant, butterfly and frog metamorphosis, magnets, the human body, water, tools, and inventions.

Fun Features

Some poems can be sung to familiar songs. Others are good for hand clapping, jump roping, or ball bouncing. Different poetry forms are introduced in the collection, such as limericks, list poems, haiku, riddles, and concrete poetry.

What You've Got

- at least two poems for every week of the year
- sets of poems that match your first grade themes
- suggestions in the introduction for using the poems to teach high frequency words and emergent reading skills
- suggestions in the introduction for making the poems personal and interactive and for using them as creative springboards
- poetry strips and an illustration to use with the Desktop Pocket Chart

Useful Accessories

The following accessories can be useful when extending the poems:

Desktop Pocket Chart
My Very Own Poetry Collection includes strips for each poem. You can use the poems for intimate group work with the help of these small pocket charts. Most of the poems fit into the 12" x 16", 10 pocket Desktop Chart. For those poems with more lines, you can accomodate the extra line or lines by building the poem from the bottom up and leaving the first lines uncut in the top pocket. Alternately, you can use the 15 pocket Desktop Pocket Chart also available from Teaching Resource Center.

Wikki Stix
Made of waxed yarn, Wikki Stix adhere to almost any surface, including the student poem and the Desktop Pocket Chart. They are perfect for underlining or circling words in the poem with the featured phonics element.

Highlighting Tape
This removable, colorful, transparent tape can be used to highlight key words or phrases on the Desktop Pocket Chart.

Sticky Notes
Sticky notes are useful for making poems interactive. You can use them to rewrite words on the Desktop Pocket Chart.

Standard Pocket Chart and Sentence Strips
If you choose to, you can reproduce the poems on standard pocket chart strips for whole-class or group instruction.

How the Book Is Organized

Student Poems
For every week of the year you have at least two poems in large print for easy reading. You can make a copy of the poem for each child. Each child can have his or her own personal poetry collection.

Strips for the Desktop Pocket Chart
You've got all the tools you need for group work. Copy the enlarged strips (starting on page 117) onto index tag, cut them apart (for poems over 10 lines, see page 4, Desktop Pocket Chart information), and display them in the Desktop Pocket Chart. That way, you'll have a poem for many eyes to see. Groups of children can interact with the poem using this intimate, yet practical medium. You can also copy the illustration to use with the strips.

Poetry Posters
You can enlarge the poems to poster size (11" x14" @130%) using a copier that allows for this. You may want to ask for assistance at your local copy center.

Suggestions for Going Further
The introduction (pp. 3–16) provides an extensive array of activities that will help you get the most from the poetry. The suggestions show how you can use the poems to focus on high frequency words, phonograms and other phonemic elements, rhyming words, repetitive phrases, and other treasures buried in the poems. The suggestions also include ideas for making the poems personal and interactive for the children and for tapping children's own poetic talents.

How to Use the Elements of the Book

There are many ways to use the personal poetry collection with your students.

Ways to Use the Student Poems
- photocopy the poem for each child
- enjoy the poem for the beauty of the words, the rhythm, and the content
- add blanks to the poem by covering certain words so that children can interact with it and personalize it
- use the poem to point out high frequency words, phonograms, short and long vowel sounds, r-controlled vowels, consonant digraphs, and more
- have each child create a personal poetry collection with a decorated cover
- enlarge the poem to 11" by 14" and use it as a poem poster in the classroom
- when the collection is complete, send it home to be read with family members

Suggestions for Going Further with the Student Poems

Timeline of Me

First tooth
First words
First steps
First trike
First pup
First book
FIRST TOOTH OUT!
First bike

Talk about the title. The title can be a very important part of the poem. Let children predict what the poem will be about.

My Face

My face shows feelings,
and that isn't bad.

I can't hide sad.
I can't hide mad.
And I really, really
can't hide glad!

Have children circle or underline the words in poem that include the phonogram you are studying.

I'm in a Bubble in My Dream

I fly by a dog.
I fly by a cat.
I fly by a rose.
Now how about that?

I fly by a weed.
I fly by a pine.
I land on a soft,
white dandelion.

Invite children to underline the repetitive words or phrases in the poem.

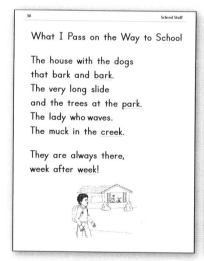

What I Pass on the Way to School

The house with the dogs
that bark and bark.
The very long slide
and the trees at the park.
The lady who waves.
The muck in the creek.

They are always there,
week after week!

Work together to find the rhyming words and underline them. Emphasize them as you're reading the poem aloud.

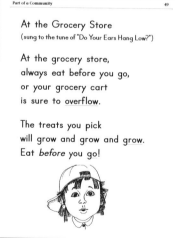

At the Grocery Store
(sung to the tune of "Do Your Ears Hang Low?")

At the grocery store,
always eat before you go,
or your grocery cart
is sure to overflow.

The treats you pick
will grow and grow and grow.
Eat before you go!

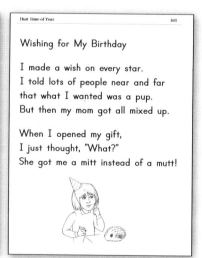

Wishing for My Birthday

I made a wish on every star.
I told lots of people near and far
that what I wanted was a pup.
But then my mom got all mixed up.

When I opened my gift,
I just thought, "What?"
She got me a mitt instead of a mutt!

Talk about the humor in the poem or the twist at the end.

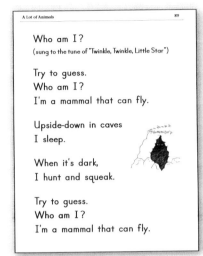

A Lot of Animals   89

Who am I?
(sung to the tune of "Twinkle, Twinkle, Little Star")

Try to guess.
Who am I?
I'm a mammal that can fly.

Upside-down in caves
I sleep.

When it's dark,
I hunt and squeak.

Try to guess.
Who am I?
I'm a mammal that can fly.

Have fun guessing the answers to the riddles about a bat, a penny, and a wheel.

School Stuff   39

Pajama Day at School

Mine had dogs.
Jay's had jeeps.

Missy had slippers with big white sheep.

Tim had a robe.
Molly had a cap.
Sammy lay down
and took a nap!

Clap to the rhythm of the poem.

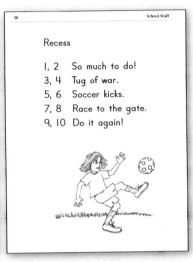

38   School Stuff

Recess

1, 2   So much to do!
3, 4   Tug of war.
5, 6   Soccer kicks.
7, 8   Race to the gate.
9, 10   Do it again!

Enjoy the chants by clapping, jumping rope, or bouncing a ball.

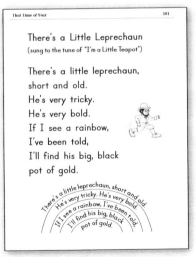

That Time of Year   101

There's a Little Leprechaun
(sung to the tune of "I'm a Little Teapot")

There's a little leprechaun,
short and old.
He's very tricky.
He's very bold.
If I see a rainbow,
I've been told,
I'll find his big, black
pot of gold.

There's a little leprechaun, short and old.
He's very tricky. He's very bold.
If I see a rainbow, I've been told.
I'll find his big, black
pot of gold.

Have individuals, partners, or groups recite the poem to develop oral literacy. Or have everyone memorize the poem and recite it together.

Have children read the poem with an older buddy, taking turns reading every other line.

Sing along to the poems that go with familiar melodies:

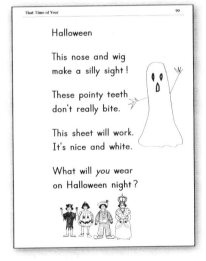

That Time of Year   99

Halloween

This nose and wig
make a silly sight!

These pointy teeth
don't really bite.

This sheet will work.
It's nice and white.

What will *you* wear
on Halloween night?

Invite children to make a border for the poem or an additional illustration.

I'm Glad I Can Bend 73

I'm Glad We Can Bend

If we didn't have elbows,
it would be hard to eat
an ice cream cone or a popcorn treat.

If we didn't have knees,
it would be hard to run
or skip or jump or race for fun.

If we didn't have waists
it would be hard to sit.
I'm glad we can bend.
Think about it!

Help children write a new verse. New verses don't have to rhyme.

Examples:

If we didn't have wrists,
it would be hard to
throw a Frisbee or a baseball.

If we didn't have ankles,
it would be hard to jump
and play soccer.

If we didn't have finger joints,
it would be hard to write
and tie shoes.

40 School Stuff

I Wish

I wish all my friends
were in my class.

I wish that recess
would last and last.

I wish the school
was next to my house.

I wish I could keep
our classroom mouse!

I wish I had all the video games
in the world.

I wish I could go up in a rocket ship.

I wish I had my own room

Maybe I'll get my wishes soon.

80 Science Poems

BUTTERFLY acrostic

Begin as a tiny caterpillar.
Up and down, you move on the ground.
Time to eat. Munch. Munch.
Then leave your skin all around.
Enough of that. Spin a cocoon.
Relax and do your springtime thing.
Finally, it's time to
Let yourself out.
You're beautiful! Look at those wings!

92 A Lot of Animals

Sounds in the Woods
haiku

Rat-a-tat-a-tat
Woodpecker loudly pecking.
What does the tree think?

Grrowl, grrowl, grrrr
Brown bear cubs playing around
in the dry fall leaves.

Tappity-tap-tap
Two deer running through the woods.
They saw us coming.

As a class, write a new poem using the original as a model. Shown here is an acrostic poem. Children can write acrostic poems about such topics as a sport, an animal, or a season.

Have children write poems modeled after the above haiku. Possible topics are barking dogs, chattering squirrels, elephants squirting water, crowing roosters, and snorting pigs.

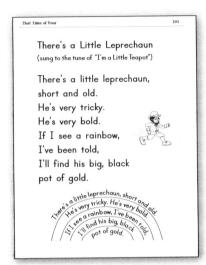

That Time of Year   101

There's a Little Leprechaun
(sung to the tune of "I'm a Little Teapot")

There's a little leprechaun,
short and old.
He's very tricky.
He's very bold.
If I see a rainbow,
I've been told,
I'll find his big, black
pot of gold.

There's a little leprechaun, short and old. He's very tricky. He's very bold. If I see a rainbow, I've been told, I'll find his big, black pot of gold.

Let children write a concrete poem that is inside a special shape, such as the one above. Children can write a Valentine poem in the shape of a heart, a sports poem in the shape of a ball, or a food poem in the shape of a favorite treat.

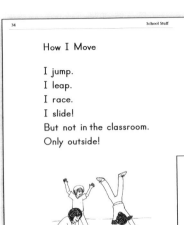

34   School Stuff

How I Move

I jump.
I leap.
I race.
I slide!
But not in the classroom.
Only outside!

Some of the poems are mostly action words. Invite children to write poems with lots of action words. Subjects might be How I Dance, How I Race, How I Play Basketball or Soccer.

How I Run

I sprint.
I dash.
I speed like a cheetah.
I gallop.
I fly!

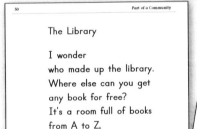

50   Part of a Community

The Library

I wonder
who made up the library.
Where else can you get
any book for free?
It's a room full of books
from A to Z,
to read by yourself
or with family!

Have children answer the questions in the poem.

Answer:
Benjamin Franklin started the first subscription library in the American colonies.

The Summer Sprinkler   97

The Summer Sprinkler

Green grass.
Hot day.
Cold water.
Let's play.
Hop, skip.
Jump, run.
Scream, yell.
Have fun.
Get ready. Get set.
We're getting all wet.

The above poem starts with describing words, nouns. It changes to action words. Have children write poems modeled after it.

The Fall Leaves

Red leaves.
Yellow leaves.
Crunch.
Rake.
Throw.
Jump.
Yell.

Answers will vary.

Goofy Poems   113

Would You Rather?

Would you rather
climb a tree or water-ski?

Would you rather
learn to sail or ride a whale?

Would you rather
fly a plane
or have a Great Dane?

Would you rather
ride a broom
or climb walls
in your room?

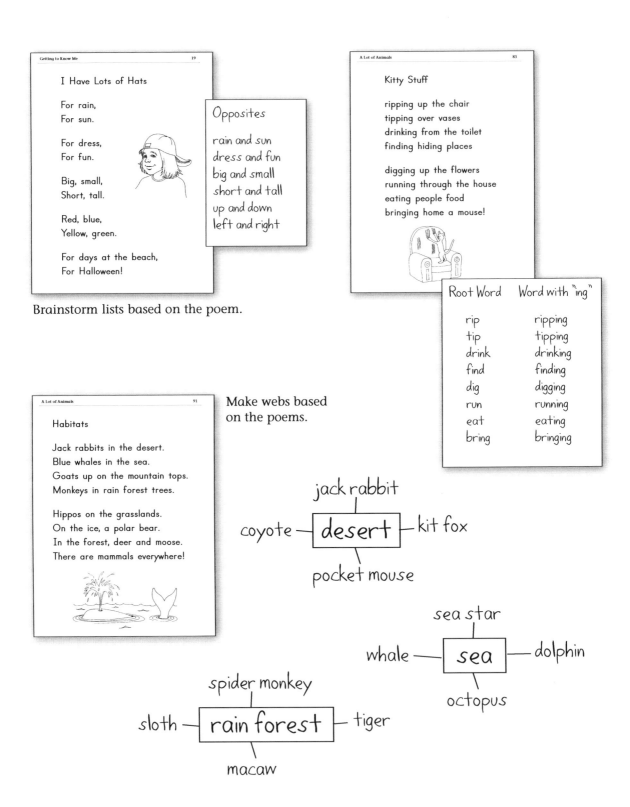

I Have Lots of Hats

For rain,
For sun.

For dress,
For fun.

Big, small,
Short, tall.

Red, blue,
Yellow, green.

For days at the beach,
For Halloween!

Opposites

rain and sun
dress and fun
big and small
short and tall
up and down
left and right

Brainstorm lists based on the poem.

Kitty Stuff

ripping up the chair
tipping over vases
drinking from the toilet
finding hiding places

digging up the flowers
running through the house
eating people food
bringing home a mouse!

Root Word	Word with "ing"
rip	ripping
tip	tipping
drink	drinking
find	finding
dig	digging
run	running
eat	eating
bring	bringing

Make webs based on the poems.

Habitats

Jack rabbits in the desert.
Blue whales in the sea.
Goats up on the mountain tops.
Monkeys in rain forest trees.

Hippos on the grasslands.
On the ice, a polar bear.
In the forest, deer and moose.
There are mammals everywhere!

jack rabbit
coyote — desert — kit fox
pocket mouse

sea star
whale — sea — dolphin
octopus

spider monkey
sloth — rain forest — tiger
macaw

Make a graph based on the poem.

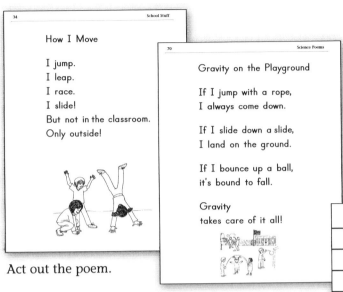

34 School Stuff

How I Move

I jump.
I leap.
I race.
I slide!
But not in the classroom.
Only outside!

70 Science Poems

Gravity on the Playground

If I jump with a rope,
I always come down.

If I slide down a slide,
I land on the ground.

If I bounce up a ball,
it's bound to fall.

Gravity
takes care of it all!

32 School Stuff

Our Names

Some names are long
like *Jessica*.
Some names are short
like *Mike*.
Some names are fun to say
like *Juan*.
Some names are just alike.

Act out the poem.

Number of Letters in Our Names					
		Luke			
		Sara	Maria		
		Noah	Kayla	Marcos	
	Ann	Emma	Kwaku	Nicole	Young-ju
Bo	Sal	Mike	Billy	Ashley	Jessica
2	3	4	5	6	7

Explore the math in the poem. After reading "When Grandma Was a Girl," compare the prices today to the prices when Grandma was a girl.

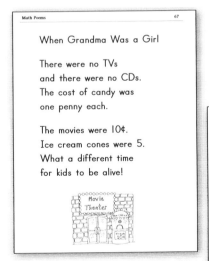

Math Poems 67

When Grandma Was a Girl

There were no TVs
and there were no CDs.
The cost of candy was
one penny each.

The movies were 10¢.
Ice cream cones were 5.
What a different time
for kids to be alive!

62 Math Poems

I Can Make a Triangle

I can make a triangle.
That's a breeze.
I can make a rectangle
on hands and knees.

My body makes a circle
if I roll into a ball.
But a six-sided hexagon?
Can't make that at all!

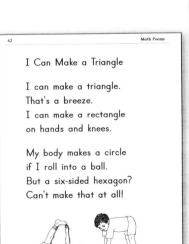

Math Poems 61

Snow People

How many balls for one snow girl?
How many balls for two?
How many balls for three or four?
That's a lot of rolling to do!

Use manipulatives to act out the math poems. Make snow people using blocks.

Have children create geometric shapes with their bodies.

Try out some of the science ideas.

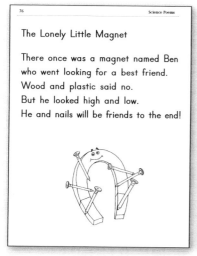

The Lonely Little Magnet

There once was a magnet named Ben
who went looking for a best friend.
Wood and plastic said no.
But he looked high and low.
He and nails will be friends to the end!

Experiment with magnets.

My Tomato Plant

It starts out as a little **seed**.
and soon it has a few green **leaves**.
Its **stem** grows strong
and tall and long.
Its **roots** all creep
in the dirt so deep.
And every place
there's a **flower**, you know,
that's a place a new **tomato** will grow!

Plant a seasonal vegetable.

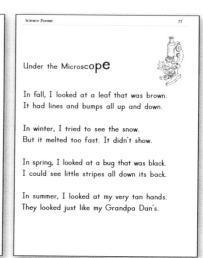

Under the Microscope

In fall, I looked at a leaf that was brown.
It had lines and bumps all up and down.

In winter, I tried to see the snow.
But it melted too fast. It didn't show.

In spring, I looked at a bug that was black.
I could see little stripes all down its back.

In summer, I looked at my very tan hands.
They looked just like my Grandpa Dan's.

Look through a microscope.

Timeline of Me

First tooth
First words
First steps
First trike
First pup
First book
FIRST TOOTH OUT!
First bike

Have children make timelines
of their lives thus far.

Do extension ideas related to
the social studies topics.

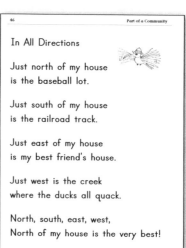

In All Directions

Just north of my house
is the baseball lot.

Just south of my house
is the railroad track.

Just east of my house
is my best friend's house.

Just west is the creek
where the ducks all quack.

North, south, east, west,
North of my house is the very best!

Have children figure out what
is north, south, east, and west
of the school.

How to Use the Desktop Pocket Chart

- Copy the poem strips and the illustration from the student poem page onto index tag.
- Cut out the strips and the illustration.
- Reconstruct the poem in the Desktop Pocket Chart. We've numbered each line to minimize confusion. You can keep the numbers or cut them off. For those poems with more lines than there are pockets, you can accomodate the extra lines by building the poem from the bottom up and leaving the first lines uncut in the top pocket. Alternatively, you can use the 15-pocket Desktop Pocket Chart also available from Teaching Resource Center.
- Gather a group of children. Read the poem once or twice for them. Track the words as you go, using a pointer or your finger. Or frame the word you are reading with a framer or your palms.
- Have children recite the poem with you, again tracking each word. Note that you may find it helpful to add and read one strip at a time.
- Work with the poem for a week. Read it together about 10 times in all.
- Place the poem in a center and have children work in pairs. They can read the poem by pointing at each word, highlighting words they know, and putting mixed-up pocket chart strips back in order.

Suggestions for Going Further with the Desktop Pocket Chart

Favorite T-Shirt

Some people wear their t-shirts out.

Some people wear them in.

And me?

I wear my favorite one

again and again and again.

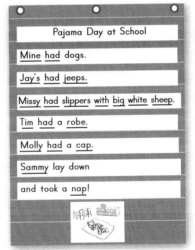

Pajama Day at School

Mine had dogs.

Jay's had jeeps.

Missy had slippers with big white sheep.

Tim had a robe.

Molly had a cap.

Sammy lay down

and took a nap!

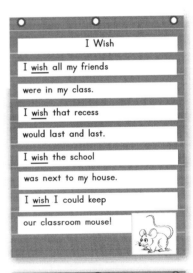

I Wish

I wish all my friends

were in my class.

I wish that recess

would last and last.

I wish the school

was next to my house.

I wish I could keep

our classroom mouse!

Birds and Cows

Birds come in flocks.

Cows come in herds.

I think I'd rather

fly and chirp

than chew my cud,

eat grass, and burp.

Use nonpermanent markers, Wikki Stix, or highlighting tape to highlight the high frequency words in the poem. They are old friends. Practice the unfamiliar words before reading the poem together.

Let children highlight the words in the poem that contain a phonemic element you are studying. "Pajama Day at School" has many short and long vowels. "I Wish" has the consonant digraph *sh*. "Birds and Cows" has many r-controlled vowels. So does "The Wind" on page 104.

I Can't
I can't.
I couldn't.
I won't.
I shouldn't.
Oh well, okay...
I'll count to five.
And then I'll try
a backward
dive!

Spring
As winter melts,
spring comes in.
on rainbows and on ladybug toes.
As winter melts,
spring flies in
on robin wings and kites on string.
As winter melts,
spring blows in
on a wind that lets warm days begin.

I Can
I can make
some paper planes.
I can teach
my cockatoo.
I can swim
way under water.
What about you?
What can you do?

Highlight contractions in the poems and figure out what two words they stand for. The poems "I Can't" and "My Face" have many contractions.

Encourage children to discover the repetitive words or phrases in the poem. Highlight them.

Have children sound out challenging words in the poems. The illustrations can help in this process.

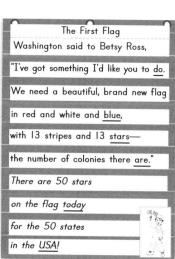

The First Flag
Washington said to Betsy Ross,
"I've got something I'd like you to do.
We need a beautiful, brand new flag
in red and white and blue,
with 13 stripes and 13 stars—
the number of colonies there are."
There are 50 stars
on the flag today
for the 50 states
in the USA!

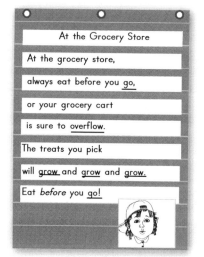

At the Grocery Store
At the grocery store,
always eat before you go,
or your grocery cart
is sure to overflow.
The treats you pick
will grow and grow and grow.
Eat before you go!

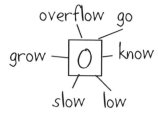

overflow   go

grow — O — know

slow   low

Have children find the rhyming words and highlight them with Wikki Stix or highlighter tape. Emphasize them as you're reading the poem aloud.

Make lists or webs of rhyming words on chart paper. Use words from the poem and add new ones, too.

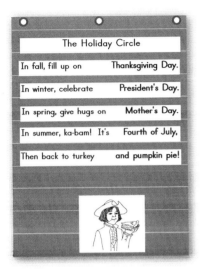

The Holiday Circle

In fall, fill up on	Thanksgiving Day.
In winter, celebrate	President's Day.
In spring, give hugs on	Mother's Day.
In summer, ka-bam! It's	Fourth of July,
Then back to turkey	and pumpkin pie!

Have fun reading the poem in two voices—reading every other part with the class. Explain that "It's my turn then your turn." The poem shown to the left is specifically written for two voices, but other poems can be easily adapted.

We Are All Special

We all have special *smiles*
We all have special names.
We all have special *families*
I'm glad we aren't the same!

Use sticky notes to cover words in the poem. Let children suggest new words to write in their places to personalize or change the poem. Alternatively, you can use blank word cards made from heavy paper to cover and replace words. (Cards should be about 2" long by 1" high.)

Valentine Presents

I gave *some fish to a cat*
I gave a bone to a dog.
I gave *some hay to a horse*.
I gave some flies to a frog.
I gave some flowers
to a bug.
And I gave my family
cards and hugs.

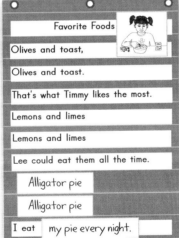

Favorite Foods

Olives and toast,
Olives and toast.
That's what Timmy likes the most.
Lemons and limes
Lemons and limes
Lee could eat them all the time.
Alligator pie
Alligator pie
I eat *my pie every night.*

Cover phrases in the poem with blank strips (find at the back of this book or purchase 1" sentence strips) and let children interact with the poem by rewriting the phrases. The new lines don't have to rhyme.

Mix up the lines of the poem and have children rearrange them. Note that this is a fun activity for a literacy center.

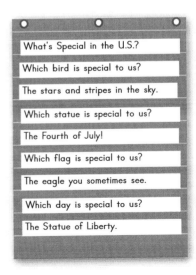

What's Special in the U.S.?
Which bird is special to us?
The stars and stripes in the sky.
Which statue is special to us?
The Fourth of July!
Which flag is special to us?
The eagle you sometimes see.
Which day is special to us?
The Statue of Liberty.

My | Cat at Night

I leave the window open.

My cat just thinks that's great.

He goes outside at 6 o'clock

and comes back in at 8.

He goes back out at 10 o'clock.

In the morning, he comes in.

He wakes me up for food and tries

to tell me where he's been.

Create word cards from high frequency words or other sets of words in the poem. Let children match them with the words on the pocket chart poem strips. This is also a good activity for center work.

at	the	open	thinks
he	and	comes	
in	out	me	been
up	for	to	where

where

Have children use letters to build a high frequency word or another word from the poem.

Enjoy the poetic elements in the poems.

The poem to the left has alliteration. The sound /b/ is used throughout.

The poem to the right has a *simile*, in the first line, a comparison of two unlike things using the word *like*.

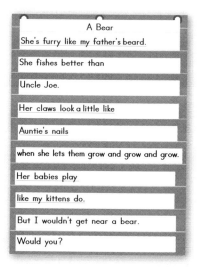

A Bear

She's furry like my father's beard.

She fishes better than

Uncle Joe.

Her claws look a little like

Auntie's nails

when she lets them grow and grow and grow.

Her babies play

like my kittens do.

But I wouldn't get near a bear.

Would you?

Bingo's Birthday

We never buy balloons.

We don't have any games.

Each year, Bingo's birthday

is always the same.

We invite Bob the boxer

and the bulldog Jake.

And we bake them a dog food

birthday cake!

The poem about a magnet is an example of personification, where an object is treated like a person.

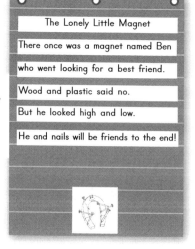

The Lonely Little Magnet

There once was a magnet named Ben

who went looking for a best friend.

Wood and plastic said no.

But he looked high and low.

He and nails will be friends to the end!

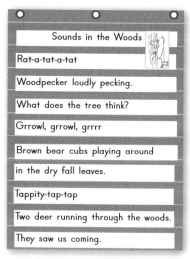

Sounds in the Woods

Rat-a-tat-a-tat

Woodpecker loudly pecking.

What does the tree think?

Grrowl, grrowl, grrrr

Brown bear cubs playing around

in the dry fall leaves.

Tappity-tap-tap

Two deer running through the woods.

They saw us coming.

The haiku above includes onomatopoeia—words that sound like what they mean.

My Shadow Is Happy

My shadow is happy
when I run.
My shadow is happy
when I play.

When the clouds come out,
It goes away.
My shadow and I
like sunny days!

My Tooth

I wiggle it up.
I wiggle it down.
I wiggle it to and fro.
I wiggle it left.
I wiggle it right.
My tooth just won't let go!

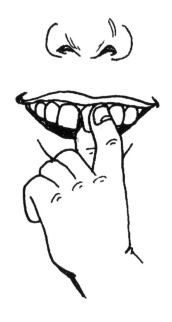

I Have Lots of Hats

For rain,
For sun.

For dress,
For fun.

Big, small,
Short, tall.

Red, blue,
Yellow, green.

For days at the beach,
For Halloween!

My Face

My face shows feelings,
and that isn't bad.

I can't hide sad.
I can't hide mad.
And I really, really
can't hide glad!

Timeline of Me

First tooth

First words

First steps

First trike

First pup

First book

FIRST TOOTH OUT!

First bike

My Favorite Sandwich

Peanut butter,
Peanut butter,
Peanut butter and jelly.

I put it in the microwave
and then into my belly.

Peanut butter.
Peanut butter.
Peanut butter and jelly!

My Quilt

I see my jeans.

I see dad's shirt.

I see my mom's old yellow skirt.

I see my coat.

I see dad's vest.

I see great-grandma's old blue dress!

I'm in a Bubble in My Dream

I fly by a dog.
I fly by a cat.
I fly by a rose.
Now how about that?

I fly by a weed.
I fly by a pine.
I land on a soft,
white dandelion.

I Can

I can make

some paper planes.

I can teach

my cockatoo.

I can swim

way under water.

What about you?

What can you do?

I Can't

I can't.
I couldn't.
I won't.
I shouldn't.

Oh well, okay...
I'll count to five.
And then I'll try
a backward
dive!

Sisters and Brothers

(Sung to the tune of "If You're Happy and You Know It")

If you happen to have a brother,
clap your hands.
If you happen to have a sister,
clap your hands.
If you are the only one,
have no sister and no brother,
if there's only you — no other,
clap your hands.

Favorite T-Shirt

Some people wear their t-shirts out.
Some people wear them in.
And me?
I wear my favorite one
again and again and again.

We Are All Special

We all have special faces.
We all have special names.
We all have special wishes.
I'm glad we aren't the same!

What I Pass on the Way to School

The house with the dogs
that bark and bark.
The very long slide
and the trees at the park.
The lady who waves.
The muck in the creek.

They are always there,
week after week!

How to Make a Class

Mix in boys.
Mix in girls.
Mix in a teacher and glue.
Mix in books,
and paper,
and poems,
and good friends,
old and new.

Our Names

Some names are long
like *Jessica*.
Some names are short
like *Mike*.
Some names are fun to say
like *Juan*.
Some names are just alike.

My Messy Desk

The frog doesn't clean up the lake.
The goat doesn't clean up its mess.
The pig doesn't clean up its pen.
But I have to clean up my desk!

How I Move

I jump.
I leap.
I race.
I slide!
But not in the classroom.
Only outside!

I Get Hurt

My fingers
get hurt on the monkey bars.
My bottom
gets hurt on the slide.
My feet get hurt
on a soccer ball.

But I love having recess
best of all.

You and Me

Friendly
Friendship
Friends

Pals
Buddies
to the end.

Getting Along

"I'm first."

"Mine!"

"Let go!"

　Those words can lead to fights, you know.

"Let's take turns."

"Let's share."

　Those words can make things much more fair.

Recess

1, 2   So much to do!
3, 4   Tug of war.
5, 6   Soccer kicks.
7, 8   Race to the gate.
9, 10 Do it again!

Pajama Day at School

Mine had dogs.

Jay's had jeeps.

Missy had slippers with big white sheep.

Tim had a robe.

Molly had a cap.

Sammy lay down

and took a nap!

I Wish

I wish all my friends
were in my class.

I wish that recess
would last and last.

I wish the school
were next to my house.

I wish I could keep
our classroom mouse!

Field Trips

We saw muddy pigs.
We saw boats and ships.
We even took some all day trips.

We made finger prints.
We made special books.
We even helped out
some pizza cooks.

The Jellybean Factory
was really great.
They didn't care how many we ate!

Over the Neighborhood

A bird flies
over the neighborhood.
Flap, flap, flap.

She looks down
on the people's homes.
It looks just like a map.

She sees the way the streets all meet.
She sees the park and all the trees.

She sees the school and tops of stores—
she sees the whole community!

My Perfect Town

A fire house,
an apple tree,
a store to rent a DVD,
an ice cream shop,
a store for candy,
and one for toys
would all be dandy.

I'd also like
a pizza place
and lots and lots
of playing space.

Guess Who I Am

I'm going around and around.
I'm rolling on the ground—

on a truck

a car

a bike

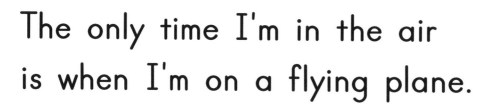

a van

a cab

a bus

and even a train.

The only time I'm in the air
is when I'm on a flying plane.

Homes

Homes can be brick.
Homes can be wood.
There are lots of homes in a neighborhood.

Apartment houses.
Trailers.
Boats.
Some people live in homes that float.

Old ones, new ones,
gray, white, red.
We all need a place
to lay our heads.

In All Directions

Just north of my house
is the baseball lot.

Just south of my house
is the railroad track.

Just east of my house
is my best friend's house.

Just west is the creek
where the ducks all quack.

North, south, east, west,
north of my house is the very best!

How I Help at Home

At home, I'm part
of a community—
my mom, my dad,
my sisters, and me.

So I set the table.
I make my bed.
And I make sure that the cat is fed.

Helpers

The teachers help
when we're at school.

The police woman helps us
follow the rules.

The librarian finds
a book that's good.

You know who fights fires
in the neighborhood!

At the Grocery Store

(sung to the tune of "Do Your Ears Hang Low?")

At the grocery store,
always eat before you go,
or your grocery cart
is sure to overflow.
The treats you pick
will grow and grow and grow.
Eat *before* you go!

The Library

I wonder
who made up the library.
Where else can you get
any book for free?
It's a room full of books
from A to Z,
to read by yourself
or with family!

Dear Mail Carrier,

You always give us letters
for my mom and for my dad.
Could you bring a few for me
and for my brother Brad?
And also if you wouldn't mind,
we'd like a box or two.
I guess if we wrote letters,
then we'd get back quite a few.

Rules on Signs

For cars, red traffic lights mean STOP.
Green traffic lights mean GO.
The yellow means GET READY TO STOP
and TIME TO GO VERY SLOW.

All over town the STOP signs tell
the cars what they need to know.
And when I cross a road,
the "WALK" means GO.
A red hand, NO!

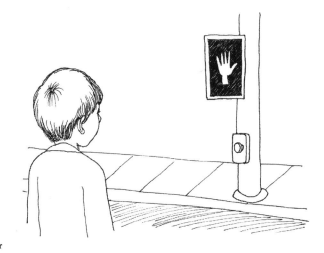

What If...

What if the mailman
kept the mail?
What if the police
slept all day?

What if the baker
ate her cakes?
I'm glad they're all doing
their jobs today!

I Live in...

I live in a home
in a neighborhood
that's in a city
that's in a state.
But I'm not done.
Now just you wait!

That state is in a country that's free,
that's in a world of land and sea.

The First Flag

Washington said to Betsy Ross,
"I've got something I'd like you to do.

We need a beautiful, brand new flag
in red and white and blue,

with 13 stripes and 13 stars—
the number of colonies there are."

*There are 50 stars
on the flag today
for the 50 states
in the USA!*

50 States

50 states,
all first rate.
Which are big?
Which are small?
Which have mountains
steep and tall?
Which have oceans?
deserts? lakes?
Which is yours?
Let's celebrate!

My State

The _____ is my state's bird.

The _____ is my state's tree.

The _____ is my state's flower.

The state of _____ is home for me.

What's Special in the U.S.?

Which bird is special to us?
The eagle you sometimes see.
Which statue is special to us?
The Statue of Liberty.

Which flag is special to us?
The stars and stripes in the sky.
Which day is special to us?
The Fourth of July!

Seven Continents

Four of the continents start with A
All four of them also end that way!
Two of them look a lot like twins:
Look how EUROPE ends and begins!

Antarctica	North America	Europe
Africa	South America	
Australia		
Asia		

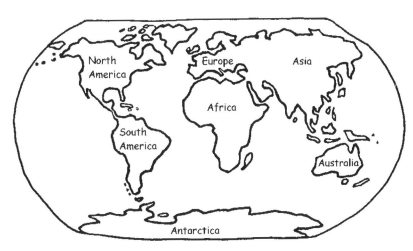

The Earth

Earth gives us air
and water to drink.
So before you waste, stop and think.

Earth gives us soil
and animals,
from rattlesnakes to bears and gulls.

Earth tells us,
"Keep the water clean.
Keep animals happy
and grasses green."

Snow People

How many balls for one snow girl?
How many balls for two?
How many balls for three or four?
That's a lot of rolling to do!

I Can Make a Triangle

I can make a triangle.
That's a breeze.
I can make a rectangle
on hands and knees.

My body makes a circle
if I roll into a ball.
But a six-sided hexagon?
Can't make that at all!

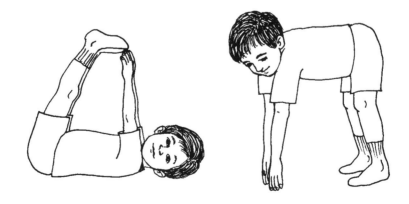

My Cat at Night

I leave the window open.
My cat just thinks that's great.
He goes outside at 6 o'clock
and comes back in at 8.

He goes back out at 10 o'clock.
In the morning, he comes in.
He wakes me up for food and tries
to tell me where he's been.

100 Days

I have a good friend.
His name is Lee Koo.
In Korea, there's something
neat they do.

When a baby gets to
its 100th day,
they have a
family holiday.

No waiting
till 365.
What is special
is 100 days alive!

My Older Brother

I am 7.
My brother is 11.
There are 4 years in between.

He'll give the top bunk bed to me
as soon as he's 18.

What is it?

I'll give you some hints:
It's metal and round.
Its color is a copper brown.

In pockets and purses
you'll find so many!
This special coin is called a _____ .

When Grandma Was a Girl

There were no TVs
and there were no CDs.
The cost of candy was
one penny each.

The movies were 10¢.
Ice cream cones were 5.
What a different time
for kids to be alive!

Giraffe Math

Giraffes must know geometry —
it's true as far as I can see.

I see some squares
and pentagons
and 2 small hexagons
at least.

Next time you see a tall giraffe,
I think you will agree with me —
GIRAFFES MUST KNOW GEOMETRY!

Numbers in My Day

7 days in one week.
9 bars on monkey bars.
3 strikes and you're out—
no matter who you are.

20 children in my class.
300 in the school.
Sometimes it seems like there are
700 playground rules!

Gravity on the Playground

If I jump with a rope,
I always come down.

If I slide down a slide,
I land on the ground.

If I bounce up a ball,
it's bound to fall.

Gravity
takes care of it all!

Seeds Take Time

If you plant a seed,
leave it alone.
It likes to grow all on its own.

I know because I dug up one
to see if all its roots
were done.

You cannot hurry a little seed.
Along with sun and water and dirt,
time is what it really needs.

My Tomato Plant

It starts out as a little **seed**.
and soon it has a few green **leaves**.
Its **stem** grows strong
and tall and long.
Its **roots** all creep
in the dirt so deep.
And every place
there's a **flower**, you know,
that's a place a new **tomato** will grow!

I'm Glad We Can Bend

If we didn't have elbows,
it would be hard to eat
an ice cream cone or a popcorn treat.

If we didn't have knees,
it would be hard to run
or skip or jump or race for fun.

If we didn't have waists
it would be hard to sit.
I'm glad we can bend.
Think about it!

Water is Cool

Water is cool.
I'll tell you why—
water can be a block of ice.
Or it can flow in a cool stream
and when it boils, we call it steam.
It's good to drink.
It keeps you clean.
And water called rain
helps the grass stay green.

Which Invention Am I?

I have a mouth.

I have an ear.

I use it when I'm trying to hear.

I have lots of buttons

like *1*, *2*, and *3*.

When I want your attention,

I never scream.

I ring and ring

till you run for me.

The Lonely Little Magnet

There once was a magnet named Ben
who went looking for a best friend.
Wood and plastic said no.
But he looked high and low.
He and nails will be friends to the end!

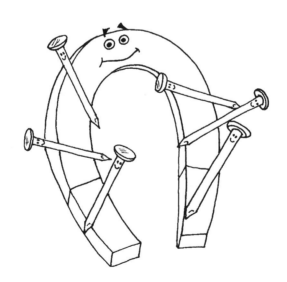

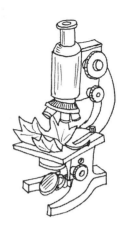

Under the Microscope

In fall, I looked at a leaf that was brown.
It had lines and bumps all up and down.

In winter, I tried to see the snow.
But it melted too fast. It didn't show.

In spring, I looked at a bug that was black.
I could see little stripes all down its back.

In summer, I looked at my very tan hands.
They looked just like my Grandpa Dan's.

Using Tools

Bam, bam. In go the nails.
I hold my hammer at the end.

Crick, crick. Take one out.
This nail always wants to bend.

Ssss, Sssss. Sandpaper's tough.
It fixes anything that's rough.

Chirp, chirp, cheep, cheep.
The birds like my birdhouse well enough!

What If You Were a Tadpole?

What if you were a tadpole,
from the very start?

What if you had a tail
and you wiggled all your parts?

What if your tail disappeared
and you grew some legs and arms?

Don't worry.
You are not a frog.
There's no cause for alarm.

BUTTERFLY acrostic

Begin as a tiny caterpillar.

Up and down, you move on the ground.

Time to eat. Munch. Munch.

Then leave your skin all around.

Enough of that. Spin a cocoon.

Relax and do your springtime thing.

Finally, it's time to

Let yourself out.

You're beautiful! Look at those wings!

My Dog Walks to School Each Day

From Monday through Friday
my dog comes each day.
Clay knows the way
and he'd just love to stay.
Some kids like to pat him.
Some kids like to play.
Even kids who pull tails
are okay with Clay.

Sharing Pets in the Classroom

If everyone's pet came
the very same day.
The pets would be going
every which way.

The snake would be
looking at the mouse.
The mouse would be hiding
in its house.

The cats would want to eat the rats.
The dogs would want to chase the cats.

Kitty Stuff

ripping up the chair
tipping over vases
drinking from the toilet
finding hiding places

digging up the flowers
running through the house
eating people food
bringing home a mouse!

Birds and Cows

Birds come in flocks.
Cows come in herds.
I think I'd rather
fly and chirp
than chew my cud,
eat grass, and burp.

Do Ants Have Ears?

Do ants have ears
to help them hear?

Do fish blink?
Do crabs have tongues?

Do frogs have teeth?
Do worms have eyes?

No they don't!
What a surprise!

Penguins

Penguins are funny birds indeed.
They slide on their tummies.
They jump in the sea.
But one thing you'll never ever see
is a penguin sitting in a tree.

Penguins stick to
the water and ground.
Penguins are birds
but they don't fly around.

A Bear

She's furry like my father's beard.
She fishes better than
Uncle Joe.

Her claws look a little like
Auntie's nails
when she lets them grow and grow and grow.

Her babies play
like my kittens do.
But I wouldn't get near a bear.
Would you?

Resting Sharks

Sharks chill out.

They slow way down.

They turn down their motors.

They glide around.

They rest and daydream

in the deep.

But great white sharks never sleep.

Who am I?

(sung to the tune of "Twinkle, Twinkle, Little Star")

Try to guess.
Who am I?
I'm a mammal that can fly.

Upside-down in caves
I sleep.

When it's dark,
I hunt and squeak.

Try to guess.
Who am I?
I'm a mammal that can fly.

Time to Go to the Zoo

Do seals have fur?
Do lions purr?
Does a baby cheetah
have spots on its back?

Do yaks really
yakkity-yakkity-yak?
Are zebras white
with stripes of black?

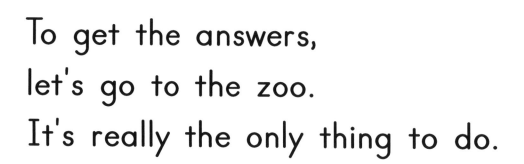

To get the answers,
let's go to the zoo.
It's really the only thing to do.

Habitats

Jack rabbits in the desert.

Blue whales in the sea.

Goats up on the mountain tops.

Monkeys in rain forest trees.

Hippos on the grasslands.

On the ice, a polar bear.

In the forest, deer and moose.

There are mammals everywhere!

Sounds in the Woods

haiku

Rat-a-tat-a-tat
Woodpecker loudly pecking.
What does the tree think?

Grrowl, grrowl, grrrr
Brown bear cubs playing around
in the dry fall leaves.

Tappity-tap-tap
Two deer running through the woods.
They saw us coming.

12 Months in a Year

January, February,
March, April, May.
Winter turns into a warm spring day.

June, July, August,
September, too.
After summer, the leaves do what they do.

October, November,
and then Decembrrrrr.
Twelve months of fun
to look back and remember.

Falling Leaves

They spin.
They fly
as they all fall down.
Let's rake a pile
on the ground.
Then run and jump
and throw them around!

Snow In California

It never snows near my house
so when we went to ski,
we took home one big snowball
and kept it under the tree.

We measured it each morning.
We watched it melt away.
When I grow up, I'm going to live
where it snows most every day.

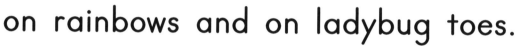

Spring

As winter melts,
spring comes in.
on rainbows and on ladybug toes.

As winter melts,
spring flies in
on robin wings and kites on string.

As winter melts,
spring blows in
on a wind that lets warm days begin.

The Summer Sprinkler

Green grass.

Hot day.

Cold water.

Let's play.

Hop, skip.

Jump, run.

Scream, yell.

Have fun.

Get ready. Get set.

We're getting all wet.

The Holiday Circle

(Read in 2 voices)

In fall, fill up on	Thanksgiving Day.
In winter, celebrate	President's Day.
In spring, give hugs on	Mother's Day.
In summer, ka-bam! It's	Fourth of July,
Then back to turkey	and pumpkin pie!

Halloween

This nose and wig
make a silly sight!

These pointy teeth
don't really bite.

This sheet will work.
It's nice and white.

What will *you* wear
on Halloween night?

Valentine Presents

I gave a cookie to an ant.
I gave a bone to a dog.
I gave some leaves to a snail.
I gave some flies to a frog.

I gave some flowers
to a bug.
And I gave my family
cards and hugs.

There's a Little Leprechaun

(sung to the tune of "I'm a Little Teapot")

There's a little leprechaun,
short and old.
He's very tricky.
He's very bold.
If I see a rainbow,
I've been told,
I'll find his big, black
pot of gold.

Father's Day—I Love You, Dad

for making cool shadows,
for turning on my night light,
for making lunches every day,
for tucking me in at night,
for clapping for my team,
for helping me ride a bike,
for buying me a catfish.

Those are things I like.

Wishing for My Birthday

I made a wish on every star.
I told lots of people near and far
that what I wanted was a pup.
But then my mom got all mixed up.

When I opened my gift,
I just thought, "What?"
She got me a mitt instead of a mutt!

The Wind

Here comes the wind.
How long will it last?
Blowing around,
it's cold and fast.

Dipping and flying,
it's twirly and curvy.
The wind makes everything
topsy-turvy.

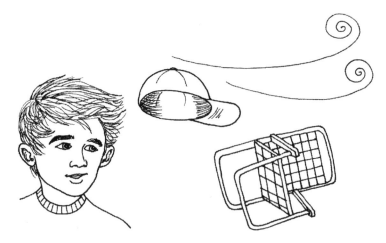

Rain

The rain can be great
on a morning in spring.
We jump in puddles
and everything.

The rain can be great
on a hot summer night,
when thunder booms
and lightning lights.

But on picnic days, it rains,
that's when rain is a real pain.

The Grocery Store at Midnight

(Sung to the tune of "The Ants Go Marching...")

The plums go marching two by two.
Hurrah! Hurrah!
The beans go marching three by three.
Hurrah! Hurrah!
The hot dogs dance with the bubble gum.
The eggs all sing
and the ice cream hums.
And the plums go marching.
The plums go marching on.

Favorite Foods

Olives and toast,
Olives and toast.
That's what Timmy likes the most.

Lemons and limes,
Lemons and limes.
Lee could eat them all the time.

Chocolate chips,
Chocolate chips.
I eat chips with hot bean dips!

Our Classroom Pig

Our class had a pig—a guinea pig.
He said "I need a fancy wig."
Well, wouldn't you know
there are no wigs
for any kind of hogs or pigs.
But then one day on "Crazy Hair Day,"
his cowlick looked the same old way.
That guinea pig won, to his surprise,
a big blue ribbon.
He got first prize!

*Read each line with an echo.
 The teacher reads the line and
 the students repeat it.

Poor Socks

My socks are not happy
with my big old feet.
Being my socks
is not a treat.

They rip. They tear.
My feet don't smell sweet—
It gets really bad
in the summer heat.

Words My Dog Knows

Sit

Walk

Bone

Squirrel

Down

Bad

Good girl!

The Lizard Olympics

Before the lizards
jump over rocks,
they stretch and get ready
with a nice, slow jog.
They race to the water
and back again.
They flip and jump
on a fallen log.

When the games are all done,
they give flies to who won.

Bingo's Birthday

We never buy balloons.
We don't have any games.
Each year, Bingo's birthday
is always the same.
We invite Bob the boxer
and the bulldog Jake.
And we bake them a dog food
birthday cake!

Would You Rather?

Would you rather
climb a tree or water-ski?

Would you rather
learn to sail or ride a whale?

Would you rather
fly a plane
or have a Great Dane?

Would you rather
ride a broom
or climb walls
in your room?

If the Beeees Agreeeed

If the bees agreed
to put their stingers away,
we could take down their hive
and play all day.

We could pat their wings and their
stripes made of fuzz.
We could make a band
and they could buzz.

Luck

Find a four-leaf clover.
Wish upon a star.
They say it's good luck
no matter where you are.

If a black cat walks by
or you walk under ladders,
they say it's bad luck.
But I don't think it matters.

My Shadow Is Happy

2 My shadow is happy

3 when I run.

4 My shadow is happy

5 when I play.

6 When the clouds come out,

7 It goes away.

8 My shadow and I

9 like the day!

My Tooth

1

2 I wiggle it up.

3 I wiggle it down.

4 I wiggle it to and fro.

5 I wiggle it left.

6 I wiggle it right.

7 My tooth just won't let go!

I Have Lots of Hats

2 For rain,

3 For sun.

4 For dress,

5 For fun.

6 Big, small,

7 Short, tall.

8 Red, blue,

9 Yellow, green.

10 For days at the beach,

11 For Halloween!

My Face

1

2 My face shows feelings,

3 and that isn't bad.

4 I can't hide sad.

5 I can't hide mad.

6 And I really, really

7 can't hide glad!

Timeline of Me

1

2 First tooth

3 First words

4 First steps

5 First trike

6 First pup

7 First book

8 FIRST TOOTH OUT!

9 First bike

1 My Favorite Sandwich

2 Peanut butter,

3 Peanut butter,

4 Peanut butter and jelly.

5 I put it in the microwave

6 and then into my belly.

7 Peanut butter.

8 Peanut butter.

9 Peanut butter and jelly!

My Quilt

2 I see my jeans.

3 I see dad's shirt.

4 I see my mom's old yellow skirt.

5 I see my coat.

6 I see dad's vest.

7 I see great-grandma's old blue dress!

1 I'm in a Bubble in My Dream

2 I fly by a dog.

3 I fly by a cat.

4 I fly by a rose.

5 Now how about that?

9 white dandelion.

8 I land on a soft,

7 I fly by a pine.

6 I fly by a weed.

1 I Can

2 I can make

3 some paper planes.

4 I can teach

5 my cockatoo.

6 I can swim

7 way under water.

8 What about you?

9 What can you do?

1 I Can't

2 I can't.

3 I couldn't.

4 I won't.

5 I shouldn't.

6 Oh well, okay...

7 I'll count to five.

8 And then I'll try

9 a backward

10 dive!

1 Sisters and Brothers

128

2 If you happen to have a brother,

3 clap your hands.

4 If you happen to have a sister,

5 clap your hands.

6 If you are the only one,

7 have no sister and no brother,

8 if there's only you—no other,

9 clap your hands.

Favorite T-Shirt

1

2 Some people wear their t-shirts out.

3 Some people wear them in.

4 And me?

5 I wear my favorite one

6 again and again and again and again.

We Are All Special

1

2 We all have special faces.

3 We all have special names.

4 We all have special wishes.

5 I'm glad we aren't the same!

1 What I Pass on the Way to School

2 The house with the dogs

3 that bark and bark.

4 The very long slide

5 and the trees at the park.

6 The lady who waves.

7 The muck in the creek.

8 They are always there,

9 week after week!

1 How to Make a Class

2 Mix in boys.

3 Mix in girls.

4 Mix in a teacher and glue.

132

5 Mix in books,

6 and paper,

7 and poems,

8 and good friends,

9 old and new.

Our Names

1

2 Some names are long

3 like Jessica.

4 Some names are short

5 like *Mike.*

6 Some names are fun to say

7 like *Juan.*

8 Some names are just alike.

1 My Messy Desk

2 The frog doesn't clean up the lake.

3 The goat doesn't clean up its mess.

4 The pig doesn't clean up its pen.

5 But I have to clean up my desk!

How I Move

1

2 I jump.

3 I leap.

4 I race.

5 I slide!

6 But not in the classroom.

7 Only outside!

I Get Hurt

1

2 My fingers

3 get hurt on the monkey bars.

4 My bottom

5 gets hurt on the slide.

6 My feet get hurt

7 on a soccer ball.

8 But I love having recess

9 best of all.

1 You and Me

2 Friendly

3 Friendship

4 Friends

5 Pals

6 Buddies

to the end.

Getting Along

"I'm first."

"Mine!"

"Let go!"

Those words can lead to fights, you know.

"Let's take turns."

"Let's share."

8 Those words can make things much more fair.

1 Recess

2 1, 2   So much to do!

3 3, 4   Tug of war.

4 5, 6   Soccer kicks.

5 7, 8   Race to the gate.

6 9, 10   Do it again!

1 Pajama Day at School

1 I Wish

2 Mine had dogs.

3 Jay's had jeeps.

4 Missy had slippers with big white sheep.

5 Tim had a robe.

6 Molly had a cap.

7 Sammy lay down

8 and took a nap!

2 I wish all my friends

3 were in my class.

4 I wish that recess

5 would last and last.

6 I wish the school

7 were next to my house.

8 I wish I could keep

9 our classroom mouse!

Field Trips

1

2 We saw muddy pigs.

3 We saw boats and ships.

4 We even took some all day trips.

5 We made finger prints.

6 We made special books.

7 We even helped out

8 some pizza cooks.

9 The Jellybean Factory

10 was really great.

11 They didn't care how many we ate!

1 Over the Neighborhood

2 A bird flies

3 over the neighborhood.

4 Flap, flap, flap.

5 She looks down

6 on the people's homes.

7 It looks just like a map.

8 She sees the way the streets all meet.

9 She sees the park and all the trees.

10 She sees the school and tops of stores—

11 She sees the whole community!

My Perfect Town

2 A fire house,

3 an apple tree,

4 a store to rent a DVD,

5 an ice cream shop,

6 a store for candy,

7 and one for toys

8 would all be dandy.

9 I'd also like

10 a pizza place

11 and lots and lots

12 of playing space.

Guess Who I Am

1 I'm going around and around.

2 I'm rolling on the ground—

3 on a truck

4 a car

5 a bike

6

7 a van

8 a cab

9 a bus

10 and even a train.

11 The only time I'm in the air

12 is when I'm on a flying plane.

1 Homes

2 Homes can be brick.

3 Homes can be wood.

4 There are lots of homes in a neighborhood.

5 Apartment houses.

6 Trailers.

7 Boats.

8 Some people live in homes that float.

9 Old ones, new ones,

10 Gray, white, red.

11 We all need a place

12 to lay our heads.

In All Directions

2 Just north of my house

3 is the baseball lot.

4 Just south of my house

5 is the railroad track.

6 Just east of my house

7 is my best friend's house.

8 Just west is the creek

9 where the ducks all quack.

10 North, south, east, west,

11 North of my house is the very best!

How I Help at Home

1 At home, I'm part

2 of a community—

4 my mom, my dad,

5 my sisters, and me.

6 So I set the table.

7 I make my bed.

8 And I make sure that the cat is fed.

Helpers

1 The teachers help

2 when we're at school.

4 The police woman helps us

5 follow the rules.

6 The librarian finds

7 a book that's good.

8 You know who fights fires

9 in the neighborhood!

1 At the Grocery Store

2 At the grocery store,

3 always eat before you go,

4 or your grocery cart

5 is sure to overflow.

6 The treats you pick

7 will grow and grow and grow.

8 Eat *before* you go!

1 The Library

2 I wonder

3 who made up the library.

4 Where else can you get

5 any book for free?

6 It's a room full of books

7 from A to Z,

8 to read by yourself

9 or with family!

1 Dear Mail Carrier,

2 You always give us letters

3 for my mom and for my dad.

4 Could you bring a few for me

5 and for my brother Brad?

6 And also if you wouldn't mind,

7 we'd like a box or two.

8 I guess if we wrote letters,

9 then we'd get back quite a few.

Rules on Signs

1

2 For cars, red traffic lights mean STOP.

3 Green traffic lights mean GO.

4 The yellow means GET READY TO STOP

5 and TIME TO GO VERY SLOW.

6 All over town the STOP signs tell

7 the cars what they need to know.

8 And when I cross a road,

9 the "WALK" means GO.

10 A red hand, NO!

1 What If...

2 What if the mailman

3 kept the mail ?

4 What if the police

5 slept all day ?

6 What if the baker

7 ate her cakes ?

8 I'm glad they're all doing

9 their jobs today !

1 I Live in...

2 I live in a home

3 in a neighborhood

4 that's in a city

5 that's in a state.

The First Flag

Washington said to Betsy Ross,

"I've got something I'd like you to do.

We need a beautiful, brand new flag

But I'm not done.

Now just you wait!

That state is in a country that's free,

that's in a world of land and sea.

159

5 in red and white and blue,

6 with 13 stripes and 13 stars—

7 the number of colonies there are."

8 *There are 50 stars*

9 *on the flag today*

10 *for the 50 states*

11 *in the USA!*

12

50 States

1.

2. 50 states,

3. all first rate.

4. Which are big?

5. Which are small?

6. Which have mountains

7. steep and tall?

8. Which have oceans?

9 deserts? lakes?

10 Which is yours?

11 Let's celebrate!

1 My State

2 The _____ is my state's bird.

3 The _____ is my state's tree.

4 The _____ is my state's flower.

5 The state of _____ is home for me.

What's Special in the U.S.?

2 Which bird is special to us?

3 The eagle you sometimes see.

4 Which statue is special to us?

5 The Statue of Liberty.

6 Which flag is special to us?

7 The stars and stripes in the sky.

8 Which day is special to us?

9 The Fourth of July!

1 Seven Continents

2 Four of the continents start with A

3 All four of them also end that way!

4 Two of them look a lot like twins:

5 Look how EUROPE ends and begins!

6 Antarctica Africa Australia Asia

7 North America South America Europe

The Earth

1

2 Earth gives us air

3 and water to drink.

4 So before you waste, stop and think.

5 Earth gives us soil

6 and animals,

7 from rattlesnakes to bears and gulls.

8 Earth tells us,

9 "Keep the water clean.

10 Keep animals happy

11 and grasses green."

1 Snow People

2 How many balls for one snow girl?

3 How many balls for two?

4 How many balls for three or four?

5 That's a lot of rolling to do!

I Can Make a Triangle

2 I can make a triangle.

3 That's a breeze.

4 I can make a rectangle

5 on hands and knees.

6 My body makes a circle

7 if I roll into a ball.

8 But a six-sided hexagon?

9 Can't make that at all!

1 My Cat at Night

2 I leave the window open.

3 My cat just thinks that's great.

4 He goes outside at 6 o'clock

5 and comes back in at 8.

6 He goes back out at 10 o'clock.

7 In the morning, he comes in.

8 He wakes me up for food and tries

9 to tell me where he's been.

1 100 Days

2 I have a good friend.

3 His name is Lee Koo.

4 In Korea, there's something

5 neat they do.

6 When a baby gets to

7 its 100th day,

8 they have a

9 family holiday.

10 No waiting

11 till 365.

12 What is special

13 is 100 days alive!

1 My Older Brother

² I am 7.

³ My brother is 11.

⁴ There are 4 years in between.

⁵ He'll give the top bunk bed to me

⁶ as soon as he's 18.

¹ What is it?

² I'll give you some hints.

³ It's metal and round.

4 Its color is a copper brown.

5 In pockets and purses

6 you'll find so many!

7 This special coin is called a _____.

1 When Grandma Was a Girl

2 There were no TVs

3 and there were no CDs.

4 The cost of candy was

172

5 one penny each.

6 The movies were 10¢.

7 Ice cream cones were 5.

8 What a different time

9 for kids to be alive!

1 Giraffe Math

2 Giraffes must know geometry—

3 it's true as far as I can see.

4 I see some squares

5 and pentagons

6 and 2 small hexagons

7 at least.

8 Next time you see a tall giraffe,

9 I think you will agree with me —

10 GIRAFFES MUST KNOW GEOMETRY!

1 Numbers in My Day

2 7 days in one week.

3 9 bars on monkey bars.

4 3 strikes and you're out—

5 no matter who you are.

6 20 children in my class.

7 300 in the school.

8 Sometimes it seems like there are

9 700 playground rules!

Gravity on the Playground

2 If I jump with a rope,

3 I always come down.

4 If I slide down a slide,

5 I land on the ground.

6 If I bounce up a ball,

7 it's bound to fall.

8 Gravity

8 takes care of it all!

Seeds Take Time

2 If you plant a seed,

3 leave it alone.

4 It likes to grow all on its own.

5 I know because I dug up one

6 to see if all its roots

7 were done.

My Tomato Plant

2 It starts out as a little **seed**.

3 and soon it has a few green **leaves**.

4 Its **stem** grows strong

5 and tall and long.

8 You cannot hurry a little seed.

9 Along with sun and water and dirt,

10 *time* is what it really needs.

6 Its **roots** all creep

7 in the dirt so deep.

8 And every place

9 there's a **flower**, you know,

10 that's a place a new **tomato** will grow!

1 I'm Glad We Can Bend

2 If we didn't have elbows,

3 it would be hard to eat

4 an ice cream cone or a popcorn treat.

5 If we didn't have knees,

6 it would be hard to run

7 or skip or jump or race for fun.

8 If we didn't have waists

9 it would be hard to sit.

10 I'm glad we can bend.

11 Think about it!

Water is Cool

1

2 Water is cool.

3 I'll tell you why—

4 Water can be a block of ice.

5 Or it can flow in a cool stream

6 And when it boils, we call it steam.

7 It's good to drink.

8 It keeps you clean.

⁹ And water called rain

¹⁰ helps the grass stay green.

¹ Which Invention Am I ?

² I have a mouth.

³ I have an ear.

⁴ I use it when I'm trying to hear.

⁵ I have lots of buttons

⁶ like 1, 2, and 3.

6 When I want your attention,

7 I never scream.

8 I ring and ring

10 till you run for me.

1 The Lonely Little Magnet

2 There once was a magnet named Ben

3 who went looking for a best friend.

4 Wood and plastic said no.

5 But he looked high and low.

6 He and nails will be friends to the end!

Under the Microscope

2 In fall, I looked at a leaf that was brown.

3 It had lines and bumps all up and down.

4 In winter, I tried to see the snow.

5 But it melted too fast. It didn't show.

6 In spring, I looked at a bug that was black. 183

7 I could see little stripes all down its back.

8 In summer, I looked at my very tan hands.

9 They looked just like my Grandpa Dan's.

Using Tools

1

2 *Bam, bam.* In go the nails.

3 I hold my hammer at the end.

4 *Crick, crick.* Take one out.

5 This nail always wants to bend.

185

6 Ssss, Sssss. Sandpaper's tough.

7 It fixes anything that's rough.

8 *Chirp, chirp, cheep, cheep.*

9 The birds like my birdhouse well enough!

1 What If You Were a Tadpole?

2 What if you were a tadpole,

3 from the very start?

4 What if you had a tail

1   BUTTERFLY acrostic

2 Begin as a tiny caterpillar.

5 and you wiggled all your parts?

6 What if your tail disappeared

7 and you grew some legs and arms?

8 Don't worry.

9 You are not a frog.

10 There's no cause for alarm.

3 Up and down, you move on the ground.

4 Time to eat. Munch. Munch.

5 Then leave your skin all around.

6 Enough of that. Spin a cocoon.

7 Relax and do your springtime thing.

8 Finally, it's time to

9 Let yourself out.

10 You're beautiful! Look at those wings!

1 My Dog Walks to School Each Day

2 From Monday through Friday

3 my dog comes each day.

4 Clay knows the way

5 and he'd just love to stay.

6 Some kids like to pat him.

7 Some kids like to play.

8 Even kids who pull tails

9 are okay with Clay.

1 Sharing Pets in the Classroom

2 If everyone's pet came

3 the very same day.

4 The pets would be going

5 every which way.

6 The snake would be

7 looking at the mouse.

8 The mouse would be hiding

8 in its house.

10 The cats would want to eat the rats.

11 The dogs would want to chase the cats.

Kitty Stuff

1

2 ripping up the chair

3 tipping over vases

4 drinking from the toilet

5 finding hiding places

6 digging up the flowers

7 running through the house

8 eating people food

9 bringing home a mouse!

1 Birds and Cows

2 Birds come in flocks.

3 Cows come in herds.

4 I think I'd rather

5 fly and chirp

6 than chew my cud,

7 eat grass, and burp.

Do Ants Have Ears ?

2 Do ants have ears

3 to help them hear ?

4 Do fish blink?

5 Do crabs have tongues ?

6 Do frogs have teeth ?

7 Do worms have eyes ?

8 No they don't !

9 What a surprise !

1 Penguins

2 Penguins are funny birds indeed.

3 They slide on their tummies.

4 They jump in the sea.

5 But one thing you'll never ever see

6 is a penguin sitting in a tree.

7 Penguins stick to

8 the water and ground.

9 Penguins are birds

10 but they don't fly around.

A Bear

2 She's furry like my father's beard.

3 She fishes better than

4 Uncle Joe.

5 Her claws look a little like

6 Auntie's nails

7 when she lets them grow and grow and grow.

8 Her babies play

9 like my kittens do.

10 But I wouldn't get near a bear.

11 Would you?

Resting Sharks

2 Sharks chill out.

3 They slow way down.

4 They turn down their motors.

5 They glide around.

6 They rest and daydream

7 in the deep.

8 But great white sharks never sleep.

Who am I ?

1

2 Try to guess.

3 Who am I ?

4 I'm a mammal that can fly.

5 Upside-down in caves

198

6 I sleep.

7 When it's dark,

8 I hunt and squeak.

9 Try to guess.

10 Who am I ?

11 I'm a mammal that can fly.

1 Time to Go to the Zoo

2 Do seals have fur?

3 Do lions purr?

4 Does a baby cheetah

5 have spots on its back?

6 Do yaks really

7 yakkity-yakkity-yak?

8 Are zebras white

9 with stripes of black?

10 To get the answers,

11 let's go to the zoo.

12 It's really the only thing to do.

Habitats

2 Jack rabbits in the desert.

3 Blue whales in the sea.

4 Goats up on the mountain tops.

5 Monkeys in rain forest trees.

6 Hippos on the grasslands.

7 On the ice, a polar bear.

8 In the forest, deer and moose.

9 There are mammals everywhere!

1 Sounds in the Woods

2 Rat-a-tat-a-tat

3 Woodpecker loudly pecking.

4 What does the tree think?

5 Grrowl, grrowl, grrrr

6 Brown bear cubs playing around

7 in the dry fall leaves.

8 Tappity-tap-tap

9 Two deer running through the woods.

10 They saw us coming.

1 12 Months in a Year

2 January, February,

3 March, April, May.

4 Winter turns into a warm spring day.

5 June, July, August,

6 September, too.

7 After summer, the leaves do what they do.

8 October, November,

9 and then Decembrrrrrr.

10 Twelve months of fun

11 to look back and remember.

Falling Leaves

2 They spin.

3 They fly

4 as they all fall down.

5 Let's rake a pile

6 on the ground.

7 Then run and jump

8 and throw them around!

Snow In California

1

2 It never snows near my house

3 so when we went to ski,

4 we took home one big snowball

5 and kept it under the tree.

6 We measured it each morning.

7 We watched it melt away.

8 When I grow up, I'm going to live

9 where it snows most every day.

1 Spring

2 As winter melts,

3 spring comes in.

4 on rainbows and on ladybug toes.

5 As winter melts,

6 spring flies in

7 on robin wings and kites on string.

8 As winter melts,

9 spring blows in

10 on a wind that lets warm days begin.

1 The Summer Sprinkler

2 Green grass.

3 Hot day.

4 Cold water.

5 Let's play.

6 Hop, skip.

7 Jump, run.

8 Scream, yell.

9 Have fun.

10 Get ready. Get set.

11 We're getting all wet.

The Holiday Circle

2 In fall, fill up on Thanksgiving Day.

3 In winter, celebrate President's Day.

4 In spring, give hugs on Mother's Day.

5 In summer, ka-bam! It's Fourth of July,

6 Then back to turkey and pumpkin pie!

Halloween

1

2 This nose and wig

3 make a silly sight !

4 These pointy teeth

5 don't really bite.

6 This sheet will work.

7 It's nice and white.

8 What will you wear

9 on Halloween night?

1 Valentine Presents

2 I gave a cookie to an ant.

3 I gave a bone to a dog.

4 I gave some leaves to a snail.

5 I gave some flies to a frog.

6 I gave some flowers

7 to a bug.

8 And I gave my family

9 cards and hugs.

1 There's a Little Leprechaun

2 There's a little leprechaun,

1 Father's Day—I Love You, Dad

3 short and old.

4 He's very tricky.

5 He's very bold.

6 If I see a rainbow,

7 I've been told,

8 I'll find his big, black

9 pot of gold.

2 for making cool shadows,

3 for turning on my night light,

4 for making lunches every day,

5 for tucking me in at night,

6 for clapping for my team,

7 for helping me ride a bike,

8 for buying me a catfish.

9 Those are things I like.

Wishing for My Birthday

1

2 I made a wish on every star.

3 I told lots of people near and far

4 that what I wanted was a pup.

5 But then my mom got all mixed up.

6 When I opened my gift,

7 I just thought, "What ?"

8 She got me a mitt instead of a mutt!

The Wind

2 Here comes the wind.

3 How long will it last?

4 Blowing around,

5 it's cold and fast.

6 Dipping and flying,

7 it's twirly and curvy.

8 The wind makes everything

9 topsy-turvy.

Rain

1

2 The rain can be great

3 on a morning in spring.

4 We jump in puddles

5 and everything.

6 The rain can be great

7 on a hot summer night,

8 when thunder booms

9 and lightning lights.

10 But on picnic days, it rains,

11 that's when rain is a real pain.

1 The Grocery Store at Midnight

2 The plums go marching two by two.

3 Hurrah! Hurrah!

4 The beans go marching three by three.

5 Hurrah! Hurrah!

6 The hot dogs dance with the bubble gum.

7 The eggs all sing

8 and the ice cream hums.

9 And the plums go marching.

10 The plums go marching on.

1 Favorite Foods

2 Olives and toast,

3 Olives and toast.

4 That's what Timmy likes the most.

5 Lemons and limes,

6 Lemons and limes.

7 Lee could eat them all the time.

8 Chocolate chips,

9 Chocolate chips.

10 I eat chips with hot bean dips!

Our Classroom Pig

2 Our class had a pig—a guinea pig.

3 He said "I need a fancy wig."

4 Well, wouldn't you know

5 there are no wigs

6 for any kind of hogs or pigs.

7 But then one day on "Crazy Hair Day,"

8 his cowlick looked the same old way.

9 That guinea pig won, to his surprise,

10 a big blue ribbon.

11 He got first prize!

Poor Socks

2 My socks are not happy

3 with my big old feet.

4 Being my socks

5 is not a treat.

1 Words My Dog Knows

2 Sit

3 Walk

4 Bone

6 They rip. They tear.

7 My feet don't smell sweet—

8 It gets really bad

9 in the summer heat.

5 Squirrel

6 Down

7 Bad

8 Good girl !

1 The Lizard Olympics

2 Before the lizards

3 jump over rocks,

4 they stretch and get ready

224

5 with a nice, slow jog.

6 They race to the water

7 and back again.

8 They flip and jump

9 on a fallen log.

10 When the games are all done,

11 they give flies to who won.

1 Bingo's Birthday

2 We never buy balloons.

3 We don't have any games.

4 Each year, Bingo's birthday

5 is always the same.

6 We invite Bob the boxer

7 and the bulldog Jake.

8 And we bake them a dog food

9 birthday cake!

Would You Rather ?

2 Would you rather

3 climb a tree or water-ski ?

4 Would you rather

5 learn to sail or ride a whale ?

6 Would you rather

7 fly a plane

8 or have a Great Dane ?

9 Would you rather

10 ride a broom

11 or climb walls

12 in your room?

1 If the Beeees Agreeeed

2 If the bees agreed

3 to put their stingers away,

4 we could take down their hive

5 and play all day.

6 We could pat their wings and their

7 stripes made of fuzz.

8 We could make a band

9 and they could buzz.

1 Luck

2 Find a four-leaf clover.

3 Wish upon a star.

4 They say it's good luck

5 no matter where you are.

6 If a black cat walks by

7 or you walk under ladders,

8 they say it's bad luck.

9 But I don't think it matters.

Made in the USA
Lexington, KY
29 January 2011